D1632171

# PINNER PARK MIDDLE SCHOOL
MELBOURNE AVENUE
PINNER, MIDDLESEX
HA5 5TJ
Tel: 020 8863 1239
Fax: 020 8424 8618

11101

# Skellig

## THE PLAY

From the original novel *Skellig* first published by Hodder Children's Books,
1998. First published in play form by Hodder Children's Books, 2003.
First performed by the Young Vic Theatre Company in November 2003.
First published in the Hodder Literature series, 2005, by Hodder Murray,
an imprint of Hodder Education, a member of the Hodder Headline Group,
338 Euston Road, London NW1 3BH.

Impression number    10  9  8  7  6  5  4  3  2  1
Year                          2010  2009  2008  2007  2006  2005

ISBN-10   0 340 90555 7
ISBN-13   9 780340 905555

A catalogue record for this title is available from the British Library

Cover illustration by Cherri Coloured Funk.
Typeset in Bembo by Servis Filmsetting Limited, Manchester.
Printed in Great Britain by CPI Bath.

Orders: please contact Bookpoint Ltd, 130 Milton Park, Abingdon, Oxon
OX14 4SB. Telephone: (44) 01235 827720. Fax: (44) 01235 400454. Lines are
open from 9.00 am to 6.00 pm, Monday to Saturday, with a 24-hour message
answering service. Visit our website at www.hoddereducation.co.uk

# David Almond

## Skellig
## The Play

**HODDER LITERATURE**

www.hodderliterature.co.uk

Other titles in the Hodder Literature series:

*The Fire-Eaters* by David Almond
(ISBN 0 340 88349 9)

*Kit's Wilderness* by David Almond
(ISBN 0 340 88350 2)

*Secret Heart* by David Almond
(ISBN 0 340 88351 0)

*Skellig* by David Almond
(ISBN 0 340 90554 9)

*Saffy's Angel* by Hilary McKay
(ISBN 0 340 89987 5)

*Control-Shift* by Nick Manns
(ISBN 0 340 89986 7)

*Stratford Boys* by Jan Mark
(ISBN 0 340 88354 5)

*Mondays are Red* by Nicola Morgan
(ISBN 0 340 88353 7)

*Shadow of the Beast* by Maggie Pearson
(ISBN 0 340 89988 3)

*Bad Alice: In the Shadow of the Red Queen* by Jean Ure
(ISBN 0 340 88357 X)

To order *Skellig: The Play* or any of the other books
in the Hodder Literature series, please contact
Bookpoint on 01235 827720.

*Skellig: The Play* was first performed on
21st November 2003 at the Young Vic,
66 The Cut, London SE1.

Direction – Trevor Nunn
Design – John Napier
Lighting – Howard Harrison
Music – Shaun Davey
Sound – Fergus O'Hare
Costumes – Elise Napier
Movement – Kate Flatt

Cast in alphabetical order:

Coot – Ashley Artus
Mum – Cathryn Bradshaw
Dad – Antony Byrne
Miss Clarts/Lucy Carr – Sarah Cattle
Mrs McKee – Noma Dumezweni
Mina – Akiya Henry
Dr MacNabola/Rasputin – William Osborne
Skellig – David Threlfall
Michael – Kevin Wathen
Leaky – Mo Zainal

Understudies – Chris Lennon & Cherry Menlove

# CHARACTERS
## (in order of appearance)

Mr Stone
Dad
Mum
Michael
Skellig
Rasputin
The Yeti
Miss Clarts
Leakey
Coot
Mina
Lucy Carr
Nurse
Old Woman
Dr MacNabola
Mrs McKee

# ACT ONE

1

*A dilapidated house in Falconer Road. Day.*

| | |
|---|---|
| **STONE** | Here it is, then, |
| **NARRATION** | Said the estate agent, Mr Stone. |
| **STONE** | Number 15, Falconer Road. Just imagine what you could do. |
| **DAD** | It'll be an adventure, |
| **NARRATION** | Said Michael's dad. |
| **MUM** | Oh, my goodness! |
| **NARRATION** | Said his mum. |
| **STONE** | See it with your mind's eye. |
| **NARRATION** | Michael just wanted to get out, to get back to the old house in Random Road. |
| **NARRATION** | He kept imagining the old man, Ernie Myers, who'd lived here for years. |
| **NARRATION** | He'd been dead nearly a week before they found him. That's what Michael saw when Stone said, |

3

| | |
|---|---|
| **STONE** | Just imagine. |
| **NARRATION** | He even said it when they got to the dining room. |
| **NARRATION** | There was an old toilet in the corner. |
| **STONE** | Ernie couldn't manage the stairs, so his bed was brought in and . . . |
| **MICHAEL** | Is this where he died? |
| **STONE** | Died? Don't think about that, lad. Cheer up! |
| **MICHAEL** | Must have been. |
| **STONE** | Come and see this garage! |
| **NARRATION** | Garage! |
| **NARRATION** | It was more like a demolition site. |
| **NARRATION** | Could collapse at any moment. |
| **MUM** | Be careful, Michael. |
| **DAD** | It's a death trap, son. |
| **STONE** | But see it cleaned and repaired. Could be something for you, lad. A hideaway for you and your mates, eh? |

*STONE shines the torch into the garage.*

| | |
|---|---|
| **STONE** | Just imagine. |
| **NARRATION** | Michael stared into the dark. |
| **NARRATION** | His mum and dad went on like it was some big game. |
| **DAD** | I'll get that cornice back there. And dado. Aye, dado, that's the stuff. This wall, now. Imagine .it gone, love. Imagine the space we'd open up. |
| **MUM** | And there's a perfect little nursery. |
| **DAD** | I'll paint a goal for him on the outside wall. I'll put a swing up for the little'n. And a blinking pond, eh? Fish and frogs and . . . |
| **MUM** | Not too soon, though. Don't want any dangers in her way. |
| **DAD** | No, that's right, no dangers. |
| **MUM** | Could we get it done in time? |
| **DAD** | The basics definitely. It's just routine, love. I can see it all. What d'you think, eh? Eh? |

| | |
|---|---|
| **MUM** | We'd be moving just in time for spring . . . |
| **NARRATION** | They bought the house. |
| **NARRATION** | They started cleaning it and scrubbing it and painting it . . . |
| **MUM** | Ouch. |
| **DAD** | What's up, love? Love, what's up? |
| **MUM** | Oh! |
| **NARRATION** | Then the baby came too early. |
| **NARRATION** | And there they were. |

## 2

| | |
|---|---|
| **NARRATION** | It was a Sunday afternoon, |
| **NARRATION** | Just after they moved in. |
| **NARRATION** | The others were inside the house, |
| **NARRATION** | Worrying about the baby. |
| **NARRATION** | Nobody else was there. |
| **NARRATION** | Just Michael. |

| | |
|---|---|
| **NARRATION** | He shone his torch into the gloom. |

*MICHAEL shines his torch into the garage.*

| | |
|---|---|
| **NARRATION** | The timbers were rotten. |
| **NARRATION** | The roof was sagging in. |
| **NARRATION** | It was like the whole place was sick of itself. |
| **MUM** | Michael! Didn't we tell you to wait till it's safe? |
| **MICHAEL** | Yes. |
| **MUM** | So keep out! Right? Right? |
| **MICHAEL** | Yes. Right. Right right right. |
| **MUM** | Do you not think we've got more to worry about than stupid you getting crushed in stupid garages? |
| **MICHAEL** | Yes. |
| **MUM** | What is it about kids and the blasted dark? |

*MICHAEL is forlorn. MUM returns to him.*

| | |
|---|---|
| **MUM** | Oh, Michael. Sorry it's all so rotten and we're all in such rotten |

moods. You understand, though, don't you? Don't you?

**MICHAEL**  Yes.

*Doorbell rings.*

**MUM**  That'll be Doctor Dan.

**MICHAEL**  Doctor Death.

**MUM**  Don't call him that.

*She heads back to the house.*

**MICHAEL**  Doctor Death. Doctor Death.

*MICHAEL returns to the garage.*

**NARRATION**  He didn't have time to dare himself.

**NARRATION**  He switched the torch on,

**NARRATION**  Took a deep breath,

**NARRATION**  And tiptoed inside.

**NARRATION**  Something little and black scuttled across the floor.

| | |
|---|---|
| **NARRATION** | The door creaked and cracked for a moment before it was still. |
| **NARRATION** | Dust poured through the torch beam. |
| **NARRATION** | He felt spider webs breaking on his brow. |
| **NARRATION** | Everything was packed in tight. |
| **NARRATION** | Ancient furniture. |
| **NARRATION** | Kitchen units, |
| **NARRATION** | Rolled-up carpets. |
| **NARRATION** | Pipes, |
| **NARRATION** | And crates, |
| **NARRATION** | And planks. |
| **NARRATION** | He kept ducking down under the hose-pipes and ropes and kitbags that hung from the roof. |
| **NARRATION** | The floor was broken and crumbly. |
| **NARRATION** | He opened a cupboard an inch, shone the torch in and saw a million woodlice scuttling away |

| | |
|---|---|
| **NARRATION** | He peered down into a great stone jar and saw the bones of some little animal that had died in there. |
| **NARRATION** | Dead bluebottles were everywhere. |
| **NARRATION** | There were ancient newspapers and magazines. |
| **NARRATION** | He was scared every moment that the whole thing was going to collapse. |
| **NARRATION** | There was dust clogging his throat and nose. |
| **NARRATION** | He knew they'd be yelling for him soon and he knew he'd better get out. |
| **NARRATION** | He leaned across a heap of tea chests and shone the torch into the space behind and . . . |

*MICHAEL shines the torch onto SKELLIG.*

| | |
|---|---|
| **NARRATION** | That's when he saw him. |
| **SKELLIG** | What do you want?<br>What do you want?<br>I said, What do you want? |
| **DAD** | Michael! Michael! |

*MICHAEL backs out.*

**DAD**            Michael, man!

**MICHAEL**        I know. I know.

**DAD**            It's for your own damn good.

*DAD thumps the side of the trembling garage.*

**DAD**            Imagine what might happen.

*MICHAEL grabs his arm, stops him.*

**MICHAEL**        Don't. I understand . . .
                   Is she going to die, Dad?

**DAD**            Die? What do you mean, die?
                   Dan's just told us – she's doing
                   fine. They'd have her in hospital if
                   she wasn't. Wouldn't they? Well,
                   wouldn't they?
                   Come on, get that dust off before
                   your mother sees.

3

*Kenny Street High School. Day.*

**NARRATION**      Michael wanted to stay at Kenny
                   Street High.

11

**NARRATION**            He wanted to go on with his old
                         lessons,

**NARRATION**            To keep on playing football,

**NARRATION**            To stay with his best mates,
                         Leakey and Coot.

**NARRATION**            He didn't mind the journey all
                         the way through town.

*School bell rings.*
*In assembly.*

**RASPUTIN**             Come along now. Lift up your
                         hearts and voices.
                         'All things bright and beautiful,
                         All creatures great and small . . .'

*In a corridor.*

**THE YETI**             Keep to the left, you horrible
                         people!
                         Leakey and Coot! Keep your feet
                         to yourselves, you horrible pair!

*In a classroom.*

**MISS CLARTS**          And, oh, it was so sad. Poor poor
                         Icarus. He was young and bold
                         and without fear. He flew so
                         high, almost to the sun, and the
                         wax melted and his feathers fell

away from his arms, and he began to tumble through the air. He dropped like a stone past his father Daedelus into the deep blue sea . . . Now, there's a story for you, Michael.

**NARRATION**　But Michael couldn't concentrate.

**NARRATION**　Not with so much going on.

**NARRATION**　He couldn't even concentrate on football.

*A football game.*

**LEAKEY**　On me head! On me head! Yeah! It's in!

**COOT**　It's not! It didn't cross the line!

**LEAKEY**　It did, man, it did! It was miles over! Wasn't it, Michael? Michael?

**NARRATION**　He walked to the edge of the field and stared over the town towards his new home.

**LEAKEY**　What's up with him?

**COOT**　Who knows? He was always a bit . . .

**MISS CLARTS**　You OK, Michael?

| | |
|---|---|
| **MICHAEL** | Fine, miss. |
| **MISS CLARTS** | And the baby? |
| **MICHAEL** | Fine too. |
| **MISS CLARTS** | If there's anything you need to talk about . . . |
| **MICHAEL** | No. No, miss. Nothing. |

*MICHAEL runs and slide tackles COOT.*

| | |
|---|---|
| **MICHAEL** | It did cross the line! It did cross the bloody line! |

### 4

*In the garden. Afternoon.*

| | |
|---|---|
| **NARRATION** | At home, that afternoon. |
| **NARRATION** | Pigeons that are hard as stone. |

*Home, same afternoon. DAD's carrying the toilet out.*

| | |
|---|---|
| **DAD** | Hold your nose. Make a nice water feature, eh? Or a garden ornament. |

*He sits on the toilet and grins.*

**DAD**                       Hey, have a look at this. Ready?

*He picks up a carrier bag of dead pigeons, shows them to*
*MICHAEL.*

**MICHAEL**                   Yuk. What are they?

**DAD**                       Dead pigeons. Found them
                              behind that old gas fire. Look at
                              this one.

*It's hard and black.*

**MICHAEL**                   That's a pigeon?

**DAD**                       Aye. Been there a long time, that's
                              all. Nearly a fossil. Feel it. Go on,
                              it's OK.

**MICHAEL**                   It's hard as stone.

**DAD**                       That's right. Hard as stone and
                              black as blinking coal. School was
                              OK?

**MICHAEL**                   Aye. Leakey and Coot said they
                              might come over on Sunday.

**DAD**                       Great! Just what you need.

*MICHAEL continues to inspect the pigeon in his hands. He*
*throws it up, catches it, feels its dead weight, throws it up*
*again.*

| | |
|---|---|
| **MICHAEL** | Where's the baby? |
| **DAD** | Eh? |
| **MICHAEL** | Where's Mum? Where's the baby? |
| **DAD** | At the hospital. |
| **MICHAEL** | The hospital? |
| **DAD** | Just a check-up, man. Look, I'm going to have a bath. I'll make tea for when they're back. It's routine, son. Little baby, few days old . . . 'Take me back to The Black Hills, The Black Hills of Dakota.' |

*MICHAEL crosses the garden, enters the garage.*

| | |
|---|---|
| **NARRATION** | He went out past Ernie's toilet, |
| **NARRATION** | The old gas fire, |
| **NARRATION** | The dead pigeons. |
| **MICHAEL** | I must have been dreaming. There'll be nothing there. |
| **NARRATION** | But there was . . . |

*MICHAEL shines the torch on SKELLIG.*

| | |
|---|---|
| **MICHAEL** | What you doing there? |
| **SKELLIG** | Nothing. Nothing, nothing and nothing. |

*SKELLIG pops a spider in his mouth.*

| | |
|---|---|
| **MICHAEL** | The whole place could collapse on you. |
| **SKELLIG** | You got an aspirin? |
| **MICHAEL** | An aspirin? |
| **SKELLIG** | Never mind. |
| **MICHAEL** | You're not Ernie Myers, are you? |
| **SKELLIG** | That old git? Coughing his guts and spewing everywhere. What do you want? |
| **MICHAEL** | Nothing.<br>You could come inside. |

*SKELLIG laughs but doesn't smile.*

| | |
|---|---|
| **SKELLIG** | Go away. |

*SKELLIG pops a bluebottle in his mouth.*

| | |
|---|---|
| **MICHAEL** | Is there something I could bring you? |

17

| | |
|---|---|
| **SKELLIG** | An aspirin. |
| **MICHAEL** | Something you'd like to eat? |
| **SKELLIG** | 27 and 53. |
| **MICHAEL** | What? |
| **SKELLIG** | 27 and 53. Nothing. Go away. Go away. |

*MICHAEL backs away, out of the garage, into the light. He is stunned by the light. In the distance, DAD sings 'The Black Hills of Dakota'. MINA appears, over the wall into the back lane.*

| | |
|---|---|
| **MINA** | Are you the new boy here? Are you the new boy? |
| **MICHAEL** | Yes. |
| **MINA** | I'm Mina . . . Well? |
| **MICHAEL** | Well what? |
| **MINA** | I'm Mina, you're . . . |
| **MICHAEL** | I'm Michael. |
| **MINA** | Well done. |

*MINA jumps back down into the lane.*

**MINA**               Nice to meet you, Michael.

*MINA runs away.*

5

*Inside the house. Afternoon. DAD's looking for something
to make tea. He finds a Chinese takeaway menu.*

**DAD**                No bread. No blooming eggs.
                       Can't even make me baked bean
                       special. I know, let's have a
                       takeaway, eh? We'll get it in for
                       when your mum gets back. What
                       d'you fancy?

**MICHAEL**            27 and 53!

**DAD**                Now that's clever. You did that
                       without looking. What's your
                       next trick?

*DAD writes the order down.*

**DAD**                Special chow mein for Mum,
                       spring rolls and pork char sui for
                       you, beef and mushrooms for me,
                       crispy seaweed and prawn
                       crackers for the baby. And if she
                       won't eat them, we will, and
                       serve her right, eh? She'll be back
                       on boring mother's milk again.

| | |
|---|---|
| **NARRATION** | Off Michael went to get the food. |
| **NARRATION** | Back came Mum and the baby. |
| **NARRATION** | And the baby seemed well. |
| **MUM** | Hello! We're home again! |

*MICHAEL returns with food. They eat at the table.*

| | |
|---|---|
| **MUM** | School was OK, then? |
| **MICHAEL** | Aye, fine. |
| **MUM** | And the journey? |
| **MICHAEL** | Fine and all. |
| **MUM** | Good lad. |
| **MICHAEL** | Is she OK? |
| **MUM** | Aye. They're keeping an eye on her, though. |

*DAD eats voraciously, swigs brown ale.*

| | |
|---|---|
| **DAD** | Champion nosh, eh? |

*He sees MICHAEL has left some food on his plate, reaches for it.*

| | |
|---|---|
| **DAD** | Aha! Extra 27 and 53! |

*MICHAEL covers his food with his arm.*

**MICHAEL**          You'll get fat.

**MUM**          Fatt*er*!

**DAD**          I'm famished. Worked like a slave
                 for you lot today.

*He reaches out and tickles the baby.*

**DAD**          Specially for you, little chick.

**MICHAEL**          Fatso.

*DAD grabs his belly.*

**MUM**          See?

*DAD dips his finger into the sauce at the edge of
MICHAEL's plate, licks his finger.*

**DAD**          Delicious. But enough's enough.
                 I've had an ample sufficiency,
                 thank you.

*DAD goes to fridge, takes out a bottle of brown ale.*

**DAD**          Now, where's that cheese . . .

*MICHAEL clears dishes, puts what is left of 27 and 53 into
the waste bin.*

| | |
|---|---|
| **NARRATION** | He put what was left of 27 and 53 in the outside bin. |
| **NARRATION** | And he saw Mina again, |
| **NARRATION** | Sitting in a tree. |
| **MICHAEL** | I'm just going out for a while! |

*No answer. MUM and DAD are engrossed in the baby.*

### 6

*In Mina's garden. Afternoon.*

| | |
|---|---|
| **MICHAEL** | What you doing up there? |
| **MINA** | Silly you. You've scared it away. Typical! |
| **MICHAEL** | Scared what away? |
| **MINA** | The blackbird. |

*She drops to the ground.*

| | |
|---|---|
| **MINA** | Never mind. It'll come again. |

*The blackbird squawks.*

| | |
|---|---|
| **MINA** | That's its warning call. It's telling its family there's danger near. |

22

Danger. That's you.
There's three tiny ones in a nest
up there. But don't you dare go
any nearer.
This is where I live. Number 7.
You've got a baby sister.

**MICHAEL**            Yes.

**MINA**            What's her name?

**MICHAEL**            We haven't decided yet.

*MINA clicks her tongue. She opens her sketch book and
shows MICHAEL what's inside.*

**MINA**            This is the blackbird. Common,
but nevertheless very beautiful. A
sparrow. These are tits. And look,
this is the goldfinch that visited
last Thursday.

*MINA slaps the book shut.*

**MINA**            Do you like birds?

**MICHAEL**            I don't know.

**MINA**            Typical. Do you like drawing?

**MICHAEL**            Sometimes.

| | |
|---|---|
| **MINA** | Drawing helps you to see the world more clearly. Did you know that? What colour's a blackbird? |
| **MICHAEL** | Black. |
| **MINA** | Typical. |

*MINA turns away from MICHAEL.*

| | |
|---|---|
| **MINA** | I'm going inside. I look forward to seeing you again. I'd also like to see your baby sister if that can be arranged. |

### 7

*MICHAEL'S bedroom. Night.*

| | |
|---|---|
| **NARRATION** | He tried to stay awake that night. |
| **NARRATION** | But it was hopeless. |
| **NARRATION** | He dreamed that the baby was in the blackbird's nest in Mina's garden. |
| **NARRATION** | The blackbird fed her on flies and spiders and she got stronger until she flew out of the tree and over the rooftops and onto the garage roof. |

| | |
|---|---|
| **NARRATION** | Mina sat on the back wall drawing her. |
| **NARRATION** | When he got closer, Mina whispered, |
| **MINA** | Stay away! You're danger! |
| **NARRATION** | Then the baby started bawling in the room next door. |
| **NARRATION** | And he woke up. |

*MUM comforts the baby. They sleep again. DAD snores. Dawn chorus. MICHAEL leaves his bed, goes to medicine cabinet, takes out a bottle of aspirin.*

| | |
|---|---|
| **MICHAEL** | Aspirin. |

*He goes to the waste bin, takes out the remnants of the takeaway meal, approaches the garage.*

| | |
|---|---|
| **MICHAEL** | And 27 and 53. I must be going crackers. |

*MICHAEL enters the garage, shines the torch on SKELLIG's face.*

| | |
|---|---|
| **SKELLIG** | You again? Thought you'd gone away. |
| **MICHAEL** | I've brought you aspirin. And look – 27 and 53. Spring rolls and pork char sui. |

**SKELLIG**          Not as stupid as you look.

*SKELLIG tries to eat but he's too weak.*

**SKELLIG**          No strength.

*MICHAEL squats beside him, helps him. SKELLIG slurps and licks and groans.*

**SKELLIG**          Put the aspirin in.

*MICHAEL puts the aspirin in. SKELLIG eats them.*

| | |
|---|---|
| **SKELLIG** | Food of the Gods. 27 and 53. Had a good look? |
| **MICHAEL** | Where you from? |
| **SKELLIG** | Nowhere. |
| **MICHAEL** | They'll clear all this out. What will you do? |
| **SKELLIG** | Nothing, nothing and nothing. |
| **MICHAEL** | There's a doctor comes to see my sister. |
| **SKELLIG** | No doctors. Nobody. |
| **MICHAEL** | Who are you? |
| **SKELLIG** | Nobody. |

| | |
|---|---|
| **MICHAEL** | What can I do? |
| **SKELLIG** | Nothing. |
| **MICHAEL** | I think my baby sister's really ill. |
| **SKELLIG** | Babies! |
| **MICHAEL** | Is there anything you can do for her? |
| **SKELLIG** | Babies! Spittle, muck, spew and tears. |

*SKELLIG **belches, gags, leans forward as if to be sick.***

| | |
|---|---|
| **NARRATION** | He put his hand beneath his shoulder to steady him. |
| **NARRATION** | He felt something there, |
| **NARRATION** | Something held in by his jacket. |
| **NARRATION** | Like thin arms, folded up. |
| **NARRATION** | Springy and flexible. |
| **SKELLIG** | Don't touch. |
| **MICHAEL** | Who are you? I wouldn't tell anybody. |

| | |
|---|---|
| **SKELLIG** | I'm nearly nobody. Most of me is Arthur. Arthur Itis. He's the one that's ruining me bones. Turns you to stone then crumbles you away. |
| **MICHAEL** | What's on your back? |
| **SKELLIG** | A jacket, then a bit of me, then lots and lots of Arthur. |

*MICHAEL tries to touch SKELLIG's shoulders again.*

| | |
|---|---|
| **SKELLIG** | No good. Nothing there's no good no more. |
| **MICHAEL** | I'm going. I'll keep them from clearing the place out. I'll bring you more. I won't bring Doctor Death. |
| **SKELLIG** | 27 and 53. 27 and 53. |

*MICHAEL leaves the garage. He feels his shoulder blades. The blackbird sings.*

8

*Kenny Street High School. Day.*

| | |
|---|---|
| **NARRATION** | Back at school. |
| **NARRATION** | An evolution lesson. |

**NARRATION**       Shoulder blades, pigs and gorillas.

*MICHAEL, LEAKEY, COOT and others are in the classroom. RASPUTIN has a poster of our ancestors, of the endless shape-changing that led to us.*

**RASPUTIN**       We start off in the primeval soup. We're little cell-like things, then fishy things, froggy things, then things that crawl out onto land. We start to look a bit like us. Ape-like things, monkey-like things. There's the main route, but there's also false tracks, wrong turnings, routes that led to nothing. Hominid. Australopithecus. Neanderthal. Homo erectus. See how we stand straighter, how we lose our hair, how we start to use tools, how our heads change shape to hold our great brains . . .

**COOT**       What a load of rubbish.

**LEAKEY**       Eh?

**COOT**       It's bollocks, man. My dad says there's no way that monkeys can turn into men. Just got to look at them. Stands to reason, man.

**MICHAEL**       Sir!

29

| | |
|---|---|
| **RASPUTIN** | Michael? |
| **MICHAEL** | Will we always keep on changing? |
| **RASPUTIN** | Who knows, Michael? Maybe we're in the process of evolving right now, but we don't know it yet . . . |
| **COOT** | Bollocks! |
| **MICHAEL** | Sir! |
| **RASPUTIN** | Michael? |
| **MICHAEL** | What are shoulder blades for, sir? |
| **RASPUTIN** | I know what my mother used to tell me, but to be honest, I haven't a clue. |

*School bell. End of lesson. COOT hunches his shoulders up and runs at the girls.*

| | |
|---|---|
| **LUCY CARR** | Stop it, you pig! |
| **COOT** | Pig? I'm not a pig. I'm a gorilla! |

9

| | |
|---|---|
| **NARRATION** | Back at home . . . |
| **NARRATION** | Poor lad. Back and forward. |

| | |
|---|---|
| **NARRATION** | Home to school. School to home. |
| **NARRATION** | Back at home, there was bad news. |

*The kitchen, that afternoon.*

| | |
|---|---|
| **MUM** | It's this damn place! How can she thrive when it's all in such a mess? Bloody stupid ruin! Bloody stupid wilderness! We should never have come! My little girl. My poor little girl. |
| **DAD** | The baby has to go to hospital. |
| **MICHAEL** | The hospital . . . |
| **DAD** | Just for a while. She'll be fine. It's routine. I'll work harder. I'll get it all ready for when she comes home again. |

*MUM fretfully packs baby clothes into a suitcase. MICHAEL watches.*

| | |
|---|---|
| **MUM** | Try not to worry, love. |
| **MICHAEL** | Mum? |
| **MUM** | Yes? |
| **MICHAEL** | What are shoulder blades for? |

31

**MUM**          Oh, Michael!

*MUM pushes past MICHAEL, then stops. She holds him and slips her fingers under his shoulder blades.*

**MUM**          They say that shoulder blades are where your wings were, when you were an angel. They say they're where your wings will grow again one day.

**MICHAEL**      It's just a story, though. A fairy tale for little kids. Isn't it?

**MUM**          Who knows? Maybe one day we all had wings and one day we'll all have wings again.

**MICHAEL**      D'you think the baby had wings?

**MUM**          Oh, I'm sure that one had wings. Sometimes I think she's never quite left Heaven, and never quite made it all the way here to Earth . . .
Maybe that's why she has such trouble staying here.

*She hands the baby to MICHAEL.*

**NARRATION**    Before she went away he held the baby for a while.

| | |
|---|---|
| **NARRATION** | He touched her skin, |
| **NARRATION** | And her tiny soft bones. |
| **NARRATION** | He felt the place where her wings had been. |

*MUM takes the baby, leaves for hospital.*

| | |
|---|---|
| **NARRATION** | Then he went to Mina. |

10

*In MINA's garden. MICHAEL stands beneath MINA's tree.*

| | |
|---|---|
| **MINA** | You're unhappy. |
| **MICHAEL** | The baby's gone to hospital. Looks like she's going to bloody die. |
| **MINA** | Die? |

*She jumps down from her tree.*

| | |
|---|---|
| **MINA** | Would you like me to take you somewhere? |
| **MICHAEL** | Somewhere? |
| **MINA** | Somewhere secret. Come on. Quickly! |

*They leave the garden, hurry towards the DANGER house.*

| | |
|---|---|
| **NARRATION** | They hurried out of the garden. |
| **NARRATION** | She led him towards Crow Road. |
| **NARRATION** | The houses were bigger and higher and older. |
| **NARRATION** | The gardens were longer and had tall trees in them. |
| **NARRATION** | She led him to a huge house with boards on all the windows. |
| **NARRATION** | DANGER was written on the door. |
| **MINA** | Take no notice. It's just to keep the vandals out. |
| **NARRATION** | She took a key from somewhere. |
| **MICHAEL** | What is this place? |
| **MINA** | It was my grandfather's. He died last year. It'll be mine when I'm eighteen. Be quick. |
| **NARRATION** | She unlocked the door, slipped inside, led him through into the deep dark. |

*MINA leads MICHAEL forward.*

| | |
|---|---|
| **MICHAEL** | Pitch black. Can't see. |
| **MINA** | Don't stop. Come on, Michael. Higher. |
| **NARRATION** | They ascended three stairways, |
| **NARRATION** | The stairs narrowed and steepened. |
| **MINA** | Keep going! To the very top! |
| **NARRATION** | They came to the final narrow doorway. |
| **MINA** | The attic. Stay very still in there. They might attack you. |
| **MICHAEL** | What might? |
| **MINA** | How brave are you? They know me but they don't know you. How brave are you? As brave as me? You have to be! |
| **NARRATION** | She led him in. |
| **NARRATION** | They were right inside the roof. |
| **NARRATION** | Light came in through an arched window. |

35

| | |
|---|---|
| **NARRATION** | They could see the rooftops and steeples of the town through it. |
| **NARRATION** | The room darkened and reddened as the sun went down. |
| **MINA** | Stay very still. Stay very quiet. Just watch. |
| **MICHAEL** | What will happen? |
| **MINA** | Shh. Just watch. Wait and watch . . . Look! Look! |
| **NARRATION** | A pale bird rose from some corner of the room, |
| **NARRATION** | And flew silently to the window. |
| **NARRATION** | It stood there, looking out. |
| **NARRATION** | Then another came. |
| **NARRATION** | It wheeled once around the room. |
| **NARRATION** | Its wings passed within inches of their faces. |
| **NARRATION** | Then it, too, settled before the window. |
| **NARRATION** | Michael didn't breathe. |

| | |
|---|---|
| **NARRATION** | Mina gripped his hand. |
| **NARRATION** | They watched the birds, |
| **NARRATION** | The way their broad round faces turned to each other, |
| **NARRATION** | The way their claws gripped the window frame. |
| **NARRATION** | Then they went, flying silently out into the red dusk. |
| **MINA** | Owls! Tawny owls! Sometimes they'll attack intruders. But they knew you were with me. |

*MINA points to a hole in the wall.*

| | |
|---|---|
| **MINA** | That's the nest. There's chicks in there. Don't go near. They'll defend them to the death. Come on! Be quick! |

*MINA leads MICHAEL down through the house and out into its garden.*

| | |
|---|---|
| **MINA** | Tell nobody. |
| **MICHAEL** | No. |
| **MINA** | Hope to die. |

| | |
|---|---|
| **MICHAEL** | What? |
| **MINA** | Cross your heart and hope to die. |
| **MICHAEL** | Cross my heart and hope to die. |

## 11

*The hospital. The baby is in a glass case.*

| | |
|---|---|
| **NARRATION** | In hospital, the baby was in a glass case. |
| **NARRATION** | There were wires and tubes in her. |
| **NARRATION** | They looked down through the glass. |
| **DAD** | She'll be home in a day or two. This is all routine. |
| **MUM** | Look at her. Don't fly too far, little chick. You can put your hand through the holes in the side to touch her. That's right. Let her know you're here. |

*MICHAEL touches her.*

| | |
|---|---|
| **MUM** | Tell her your name. |
| **MICHAEL** | I'm Michael. I'm your big brother. |

38

| | |
|---|---|
| **MUM** | Tell her you love her . . . Go on, son. Love's the thing that'll make her better. |
| **MICHAEL** | I love you. I love you. |

*MUM hugs him.*

| | |
|---|---|
| **MUM** | You getting on all right, son? Dad looking after you? Is there anything you need? |
| **DAD** | 27 and 53. |
| **MICHAEL** | Aye. 27 and 53. 27 and 53. |
| **MUM** | Look, Michael. She's smiling. Can you see? Can you see? |
| **NARRATION** | But it didn't look like a smile to him. |

### 12

*MINA's garden. Afternoon.*

| | |
|---|---|
| **NARRATION** | Mina's garden. |
| **NARRATION** | Songs and cages. |
| **NARRATION** | And beautiful ancestors. |

| | |
|---|---|
| **MINA** | You weren't at school today. |
| **MICHAEL** | I wasn't well. |
| **MINA** | Not surprising, considering what you're going through. |
| **MICHAEL** | You weren't at school either. |
| **MINA** | School! My mother educates me. We believe that schools inhibit the natural curiosity, creativity and intelligence of children. Don't you agree? |
| **MICHAEL** | Don't know. |
| **MINA** | Our motto is on the wall by my bed: 'How can a bird that is born for joy Sit in a cage and sing?' William Blake. The chicks in the nest won't need a classroom to make them fly. Will they? |

MICHAEL *shakes his head.*

| | |
|---|---|
| **MINA** | My father believed this, too. |
| **MICHAEL** | Your father? |

| | |
|---|---|
| **MINA** | He died before I was born. We often think of him, watching us from Heaven . . . |
| **MICHAEL** | Do you believe we're descended from the apes? |
| **MINA** | Believe? It's a proven fact. It's called evolution. You must know that. I would hope, though, that we also have some rather more beautiful ancestors. Don't you? |
| **MICHAEL** | Yes. |

*A blackbird sings nearby, heading to its nest.*

| | |
|---|---|
| **MICHAEL** | It was great to see the owls. |
| **MINA** | They're wild things, of course. Killers, savages. They're wonderful. |
| **MICHAEL** | I dreamed I heard them, all through the night. |
| **MINA** | Often in the dead of night I hear them calling to each other. |

*MICHAEL joins his hands together.*

| | |
|---|---|
| **MICHAEL** | Listen. |

*He blows into his hand, makes the owl sound.*

41

**MINA**        That's brilliant! Show me.

*MICHAEL shows her how to shape her hands, how to blow. She tries to make the sound. She can't, and then she can.*

**MICHAEL**        Leakey showed me. My mate at school.

**MINA**        I wonder if you did it at night if the owls would come.

**MICHAEL**        Maybe. Maybe you should try it.

**MINA**        I will. Tonight I will.

*She makes the owl sound.*

**MINA**        Brilliant! Brilliant!

**MICHAEL**        There's something I could show you as well. Like you showed me the owls.

**MINA**        What is it?

**MICHAEL**        I don't know. I don't even know if it's true or if it's a dream.

**MINA**        That's all right. Truth and dreams are always getting muddled.

| | |
|---|---|
| **MICHAEL** | I'd have to take you there and show you. |
| **MINA** | Come on, then. |
| **MICHAEL** | Not now. Got to go and get 27 and 53. |
| **MINA** | Mystery man, that's you. |

*MICHAEL stands, prepares to leave.*

| | |
|---|---|
| **MICHAEL** | Do you know what shoulder blades are for? |
| **MINA** | Do you not even know that? |
| **MICHAEL** | Do you? |
| **MINA** | It's a proven fact. Common knowledge. They're where your wings were, and where they'll grow again. Go on, then, mystery man. Go and get your mysterious numbers. |

### 13

*The garage. Just before dawn. Dawn chorus.*

| | |
|---|---|
| **NARRATION** | Just before dawn, next morning |

*MICHAEL carries 27 and 53, shines the torch on SKELLIG's face.*

**SKELLIG**          You again.

**MICHAEL**          More 27 and 53.

*MICHAEL crouches, feeds SKELLIG. SKELLIG slurps and licks and groans.*

**SKELLIG**          Food of the gods. Nectar.

**MICHAEL**          How do you know about 27 and 53?

**SKELLIG**          Ernie's favourite. Used to hear him on the phone. 27 and 53, he used to say. Bring it round. Bring it quick.

**MICHAEL**          You were in the house?

**SKELLIG**          In the garden. Watched him through the window. Found his leavings in the bin next morning. 27 and 53. Sweetest of nectars. Lovely change from spiders and mice.

**MICHAEL**          Did he know you were there?

| | |
|---|---|
| **SKELLIG** | Looked right through me, like I wasn't there. Miserable old toot. Mebbe thought I was a figment . . . You think I'm a figment? |
| **MICHAEL** | Don't know what you are. |
| **SKELLIG** | That's all right, then. |
| **MICHAEL** | Are you dead? |
| **SKELLIG** | Yes. The dead are often known to eat 27 and 53 and to suffer from Arthur Itis. |
| **MICHAEL** | Do you need anything? More aspirin? |
| **SKELLIG** | 27 and 53. |
| **MICHAEL** | The baby's in hospital. |
| **SKELLIG** | Some brown. |
| **MICHAEL** | Brown? |
| **SKELLIG** | Brown ale. Something else Ernie used to have. Something else he couldn't finish. Eyes bigger than his belly. Brown ale. Sweetest of nectars |

45

*SKELLIG belches and retches. MICHAEL shines his torch onto the bulges on his shoulders. He reaches out to touch. SKELLIG flinches.*

| | |
|---|---|
| **SKELLIG** | No. I said, no! |
| **MICHAEL** | There's someone I'd like to bring to see you. |
| **SKELLIG** | Someone to tell you I'm really here. |
| **MICHAEL** | She's nice. |
| **SKELLIG** | No. |
| **MICHAEL** | She'll know how to help you. |
| **SKELLIG** | Ha! |
| **MICHAEL** | I don't know what to do. The garage is going to bloody collapse. You're ill. You don't eat properly. I wake up and think of you and there's other things I need to think about. The baby's ill and we hope she won't die but she might. She really might . . . Mina'd know how to help you. |
| **SKELLIG** | Mina? |
| **MICHAEL** | She's called Mina. |

| | |
|---|---|
| **SKELLIG** | Bring the street. Bring the whole damn town. |
| **MICHAEL** | Just Mina. And me. |
| **SKELLIG** | Damn kids. |
| **MICHAEL** | What shall I call you? |
| **SKELLIG** | Eh? |
| **MICHAEL** | What should I tell her you're called? |
| **SKELLIG** | Mr Nobody. Mr Bones and Mr Had Enough and Mr Arthur Itis. Now get out and leave me alone. |
| **MICHAEL** | OK . . . |

*MICHAEL starts to leave.*

| | |
|---|---|
| **MICHAEL** | Will you think about the baby? |
| **SKELLIG** | Eh? |
| **MICHAEL** | Will you think about her in hospital? Will you think about her getting better? Please. |
| **SKELLIG** | Yes. Blinking yes. |

*MICHAEL moves towards the door and out of the garage.*

47

**SKELLIG**          Yes. Yes, I will.

**NARRATION**        Night had almost given way to
                     day.

**NARRATION**        He saw the owls heading
                     homeward on great silent wings.

*The hooting of owls. MICHAEL puts his hands to his
mouth and hoots.*

**NARRATION**        He seemed to see a face, round
                     and pale,

**NARRATION**        Inside the darkness of an upstairs
                     window in Mina's house.

*MICHAEL hoots again.*

**NARRATION**        Something answered.

*The hooting of owls.*


## 14

**NARRATION**        Mina's garden.

**NARRATION**        How to find the tiniest sweetest
                     noise.

*MINA's garden. Afternoon. MINA has her books, pens,
paints around her. MICHAEL approaches.*

| | |
|---|---|
| **MINA** | Not at school again. |
| **MICHAEL** | No. |

*MINA opens a book, clears her throat, recites.*

| | |
|---|---|
| **MINA** | Good.<br>'To go to school on a summer morn,<br>O! It drives all joy away.'<br>William Blake again. You've heard of William Blake? |
| **MICHAEL** | No. |
| **MINA** | He painted pictures and wrote poems. He saw angels in his garden. |

*MINA beckons MICHAEL towards her. He approaches.*

| | |
|---|---|
| **MINA** | Be quiet. Be very very quiet. Listen. |
| **MICHAEL** | Listen to what? |
| **MINA** | Just listen . . .<br>What can you hear? |
| **MICHAEL** | Traffic. Birds singing. Breeze in the trees. |
| **MINA** | Listen closer. |

| | |
|---|---|
| **MICHAEL** | My own heart! I can hear my own heart! |
| **MINA** | That's nothing. Listen deeper. Listen for the tiniest sweetest noise. |
| **MICHAEL** | What am I listening for? |
| **MINA** | It comes from above you, from inside the tree. |
| **MICHAEL** | Inside the tree? |
| **MINA** | Just do it, Michael.<br>It comes from the nest.<br>Just listen. |
| **MICHAEL** | Yes! |
| **MINA** | The chicks, Michael. You can hear the cheeping chicks. |

*MICHAEL continues to listen in amazement.*

| | |
|---|---|
| **MINA** | Their bones are more delicate than ours. Their bones are almost hollow. Did you know that? |
| **MICHAEL** | I think so. |

*MINA picks up a bone that has been lying on her books. She snaps it, shows it to MICHAEL.*

| | |
|---|---|
| **MINA** | From a pigeon, we believe. Feel how light it is. See how much air is inside. The presence of air cavities within the bone is known as pneumatisation. This is the result of evolution. Over millions of years, the bird has developed an anatomy that enables it to fly. As you know, we have not. You understand? You've covered this at school? |
| **MICHAEL** | I think so. |
| **MINA** | One day, I'll tell you about the archaeopteryx. How's the baby today? |
| **MICHAEL** | I'll see her later. We think she's fine. |
| **MINA** | Good. |

*MINA cups her hands, makes the owl sound.*

| | |
|---|---|
| **MINA** | Brilliant! Brilliant! |
| **MICHAEL** | I made the hooting sound last night. Just after dawn, very early in the morning. |
| **MINA** | Did you? |

**MICHAEL**   Were you looking out then? Did you make the owl sound then?

**MINA**   I can't be certain.

**MICHAEL**   Can't?

**MINA**   I dream. I walk in my sleep. Sometimes I do things really and I think they're just dreams. Sometimes I dream them and think they're real. Don't you?

*No answer.*

**MINA**   Don't you, Michael?

**MICHAEL**   Yes.

**MINA**   Good. You said you had a mystery. Something to show me.

**MICHAEL**   Yes.

**MINA**   Then show me.

**MICHAEL**   This afternoon, maybe. I have to go to the baby.

15

*The hospital. The same day.*

| | |
|---|---|
| **NARRATION** | The baby, the garage, school, the hospital . . . |
| **NARRATION** | Poor lad. |
| **MUM** | You look so tired, love. You two been staying up too late? |
| **DAD** | Dead right. It's been videos and Chinese every night. Hasn't it, son? |
| **MICHAEL** | Yes. |

*Michael hands the baby to Mum.*

| | |
|---|---|
| **MICHAEL** | Got to go out a minute, Mum. |
| **NARRATION** | He went out into the corridor. |

*Michael meets a nurse.*

| | |
|---|---|
| **MICHAEL** | Excuse me. |
| **NURSE** | Yes? |
| **MICHAEL** | Do you know where the people with arthritis go? |

| | |
|---|---|
| **NURSE** | Straight to Heaven, to make up for their pains on Earth. Or Ward 34, love. Top floor. Silly place to put people with bad bones that's got trouble walking and climbing stairs. But who am I to know? |

*MICHAEL goes higher. He meets an OLD WOMAN walking with a zimmer frame.*

| | |
|---|---|
| **OLD WOMAN** | Knackered! Once up and down the ward and three times round the landing. Absolutely knackered! |
| **MICHAEL** | Arthritis. |
| **OLD WOMAN** | That's right. Arthur. But I've got two new hips and I'll be dancing soon and that'll show him who's boss. |

*She jiggles in the frame as if dancing, then laughs.*

| | |
|---|---|
| **OLD WOMAN** | Daft owld biddy! |
| **MICHAEL** | I've got a friend with arthritis. |
| **OLD WOMAN** | Poor soul. |
| **MICHAEL** | What'll help him? |
| **OLD WOMAN** | Some folk swear by cod liver oil and a positive mind. For me, |

there's prayers to Our Lady, and
Doctor MacNabola with his
plastic bits and pieces and his
glue. Talk of the devil!

*DR MACNABOLA passes by with a clutch of student
doctors. He is doing his daily rounds.*

**OLD WOMAN**　　　Keep on moving. That's the
　　　　　　　　　thing. Don't let everything seize
　　　　　　　　　up.

*OLD WOMAN shuffles away, humming 'Lord of the
Dance'. MICHAEL follows DR MACNABOLA.*

**NARRATION**　　　He followed Dr MacNabola.

**NARRATION**　　　He looked inside Ward 34.

**NARRATION**　　　People were practising moving
　　　　　　　　　on zimmer frames.

**NARRATION**　　　They were calling to each other
　　　　　　　　　across the ward.

**NARRATION**　　　They were wincing,

**NARRATION**　　　And gasping,

**NARRATION**　　　And grinning.

**MICHAEL**　　　　Excuse me . . . Doctor
　　　　　　　　　MacNabola.

*DR MACNABOLA looks at MICHAEL.*

55

**MICHAEL**          What's good for arthritis?

**DR MacNABOLA**     The needle. Deep injections right into the joint . . . Then the saw. The lovely sound of steel on bone. Bits cut out and new bits put in. Stitch it up, good as new. Are you a sufferer, young man?

**MICHAEL**          A friend.

**DR MacNABOLA**     Tell your friend to come to me. I'll needle him, saw him, fix him up and send him home nearly as good as new . . .
Failing that, the advice is simple. Keep cheerful. Don't give up. Most of all, remain active. Take cod liver oil. Don't allow those joints to grind to a halt. Anything else?

*MICHAEL shakes his head.*

**DR MacNABOLA**     Then let us carry on.

*DR MacNABOLA and the students move on.*

**OLD WOMAN**        He's a bighead, but he's right.

**MICHAEL**          But he won't move. He just sits there and sits there.

| | |
|---|---|
| **OLD WOMAN** | Needs a kick up the backside, eh? |

*MICHAEL nods.*

| | |
|---|---|
| **OLD WOMAN** | So kick him up the bliddy backside. Make him dance. |

*MICHAEL hurries back to MUM, DAD and the baby. MUM has been crying.*

| | |
|---|---|
| **MUM** | You've been a while. |
| **DAD** | All those Chinese takeaways, eh? |
| **MUM** | Cod liver oil. That'll sort you out. |

*MUM reaches out for MICHAEL, holds him.*

| | |
|---|---|
| **MUM** | You're my best boy. Whatever happens, you'll always be my best boy. |

16

| | |
|---|---|
| **NARRATION** | Back home again. |
| **NARRATION** | Will Mina see what Michael sees? |

*The kitchen. The same day. DAD is decorating. MICHAEL takes a bottle of brown ale from the fridge.*

| | |
|---|---|
| **MICHAEL** | Brown ale. Drink of the gods. |

*He hides it beside the garage door. He gets his torch and Swiss Army knife and some cod liver oil capsules.*

| | |
|---|---|
| **MICHAEL** | Cod liver oil. That'll sort him out. Dad! Can I go to see Mina? |
| **DAD** | Don't worry about me. I'll do all the dirty work. You just run around and have a good time. |
| **NARRATION** | He went to Mina's door. |

*Doorbell. MRS McKEE comes to the door.*

| | |
|---|---|
| **MICHAEL** | Is Mina in? |
| **MRS McKEE** | She is. You must be Michael. I'm Mrs McKee. Mina! How's the baby? |
| **MICHAEL** | Very well. Well, we think she'll be very well. |
| **MRS McKEE** | Babies are stubborn things. Strugglers and fighters. Tell your parents I'm thinking of them. |

*MINA comes to the door.*

| | |
|---|---|
| **MINA** | We're making beasts. Foxes, fish and lizards and birds. Come and see. It's magic. |

*MICHAEL holds back.*

58

| | |
|---|---|
| **MICHAEL** | I was going for a walk. |
| **MINA** | Can I go for a walk with Michael, Mum? |
| **MRS McKEE** | Yes. But not too long or your clay'll dry out. |

*MICHAEL leads MINA towards the garage.*

| | |
|---|---|
| **MINA** | Is this the mystery? Is this what you were going to show me? |
| **MICHAEL** | Yes! |
| **MINA** | Keep going. Don't stop! |
| **NARRATION** | He led her quickly along the front street, |
| **NARRATION** | Then he turned into the back lane. |
| **NARRATION** | He led her past the high back garden walls. |
| **MINA** | Where is it? |
| **MICHAEL** | Not far. The place is filthy, and it's dangerous. |
| **MINA** | Good! Don't stop, Michael! |

| | |
|---|---|
| **NARRATION** | He led her to the garage. |
| **MINA** | Here? Just here? |
| **MICHAEL** | Yes. Yes. |

*He shows her some cod liver oil capsules. He picks up a bottle of brown ale from just inside the garage door. He takes a torch from his pocket.*

| | |
|---|---|
| **MICHAEL** | We'll need these.<br>Trust me, Mina . . .<br>I'm worried that you won't see what I think I see. |
| **MINA** | I'll see whatever's there. Take me in. |

*They enter the garage.*

| | |
|---|---|
| **MICHAEL** | Keep close, Mina. |
| **NARRATION** | Things scratched and scuttled across the floor. |
| **NARRATION** | Cobwebs snapped on their clothes and skin. |
| **NARRATION** | The ceiling creaked. |
| **NARRATION** | Michael trembled. |
| **NARRATION** | Maybe Mina would see nothing. |

| | |
|---|---|
| **NARRATION** | Maybe he'd been wrong. |
| **NARRATION** | Maybe dreams and truth were just a useless muddle in his mind. |

*MICHAEL shines the torch onto SKELLIG.*

| | |
|---|---|
| **SKELLIG** | Again. |

*MINA recoils, stifles a cry. MICHAEL holds her arm.*

| | |
|---|---|
| **MICHAEL** | I brought my friend. Like I said I would. This is Mina. |

*SKELLIG turns his eyes to MINA. MICHAEL holds up the brown ale.*

| | |
|---|---|
| **MICHAEL** | I brought this as well. |

*MICHAEL opens the bottle. He pours brown ale into SKELLIG's mouth.*

| | |
|---|---|
| **SKELLIG** | Nectar. Drink of the gods. |

*MICHAEL helps him to drink again.*

| | |
|---|---|
| **MINA** | Who are you? |
| **SKELLIG** | Mr Had Enough Of You. |
| **MICHAEL** | I saw a doctor. Not Doctor Death. One that could fix you. |

61

| | |
|---|---|
| **SKELLIG** | No doctors. Nothing. Nobody. Let me be. |
| **MICHAEL** | You'll die. You'll crumble away and die. |
| **SKELLIG** | Crumble crumble. More beer. |

*MICHAEL helps him to drink again. He shows the cod liver oil capsules.*

| | |
|---|---|
| **MICHAEL** | I brought these as well. Some people swear by them. |
| **SKELLIG** | Stink of fish. Slimy slithery swimming things. |
| **MICHAEL** | He just sits there. It's like he's waiting to die. I don't know what to do. |
| **SKELLIG** | Do nothing. |

*MINA crouches beside SKELLIG, takes the torch, stares at him, touches him.*

| | |
|---|---|
| **MINA** | Who are you? |
| **SKELLIG** | Nobody. |
| **MINA** | Dry and cold. How long have you been here? |

| | |
|---|---|
| **SKELLIG** | Long enough. |
| **MINA** | Are you dead? |
| **SKELLIG** | Kids' questions. All the same. |
| **MICHAEL** | Tell her things. She's clever. She'll know what to do. |
| **MINA** | I'm called Mina.<br>I'm Mina, you're . . . |
| **SKELLIG** | You're Mina. I'm sick to death. |

*MINA touches his hands, his skin.*

| | |
|---|---|
| **MINA** | Calcification. The process by which the bone hardens and becomes inflexible. The process by which the body turns to stone. |
| **SKELLIG** | Not as stupid as she looks. |
| **MINA** | It is linked to another process, by which the mind, too, becomes inflexible. It stops thinking and imagining. It becomes hard as bone. It is no longer a mind. It is a lump of bone wrapped in a wall of stone. This process is ossification. |
| **SKELLIG** | More beer. |

63

*MICHAEL helps SKELLIG to drink.*

**SKELLIG**  Take her away.

*MICHAEL guides MINA's hands to SKELLIG's shoulder blades.*

**NARRATION**  Michael took Mina's hand.

**NARRATION**  He guided it towards the shoulder blades.

**NARRATION**  He pressed her fingers to the growths beneath the jacket.

**MINA**  There's somewhere we could take you. It's safer there. You could just sit there dying, too, if that's really what you want.

**SKELLIG**  More beer.

**MICHAEL**  One of these as well.

*MICHAEL helps SKELLIG to drink. He drops a cod liver oil capsule onto SKELLIG's tongue.*

**MINA**  You have to let us help you.

**NARRATION**  The roof trembled in the breeze.

**NARRATION**  Dust continued to fall on them.

| | |
|---|---|
| **NARRATION** | Tears fell from Michael's eyes. |
| **MICHAEL** | Please. |
| **SKELLIG** | Where did you come from? |
| **MICHAEL** | What? |
| **SKELLIG** | You. From. |
| **MICHAEL** | Me? There. Out there. Why? |
| **SKELLIG** | Go away. |
| **MICHAEL** | Why won't you move? |

*SKELLIG sighs.*

| | |
|---|---|
| **MICHAEL** | Look at him. |
| **SKELLIG** | More beer. |
| **MICHAEL** | I hate you. I hate you! |
| **MINA** | You have to let us help. |
| **SKELLIG** | Do it. Do what you want. |

*MICHAEL and MINA leave the garage. They stand outside.*

| | |
|---|---|
| **MINA** | He's an extraordinary being. What's on his back? |

65

*They stare and wonder and are silent. The blackbird sings.*

| | |
|---|---|
| **MINA** | We'll take him out tonight. |
| **MICHAEL** | At dawn. |
| **MINA** | We'll call to each other. We'll hoot like owls. We'll make sure we don't sleep . . . <br> An extraordinary being. |
| **MICHAEL** | I'll go back to my dad now. |
| **MINA** | I'll go back to my clay. |
| **MICHAEL** | I'll see you at dawn. |
| **MINA** | At dawn. I won't sleep. |
| **MICHAEL** | I won't sleep. |

# ACT TWO

1

*MICHAEL's room, night. An owl hoots.*

| | |
|---|---|
| **NARRATION** | Michael slept. |
| **NARRATION** | In his dream he was with the baby. |
| **NARRATION** | They were tucked up together in the blackbird's nest. |
| **NARRATION** | Then he heard the owl. |
| **NARRATION** | He saw Mina in the wilderness. |

*MINA hoots. MICHAEL goes to her.*

| | |
|---|---|
| **NARRATION** | He tiptoed out to her. |
| **MICHAEL** | I didn't sleep all night. Then at the very last minute when the night was ending I did. |
| **MINA** | But you're awake now? |
| **MICHAEL** | Yes. |
| **MINA** | We're not dreaming it? |
| **MICHAEL** | We're not dreaming it. |
| **MINA** | We're not dreaming it together? |

**MICHAEL**      Even if we were we wouldn't know.

*The blackbird sings.*

**MINA**      Quickly, Michael. No time to waste.

*MICHAEL and MINA enter the garage, move to SKELLIG.*

**MINA**      You have to come with us.

**SKELLIG**      I'm sick to death.

**MINA**      You have to come.

**SKELLIG**      I'm weak as a baby.

**MINA**      Babies aren't weak. Have you seen a baby screaming for its food or struggling to crawl? Have you seen a blackbird chick daring its first flight?

*MINA puts her hand beneath his armpit, tugs at him. MICHAEL helps her.*

**MINA**      Please.

**SKELLIG**      I'm frightened.

*MINA kisses him.*

**MINA**      Don't be frightened. We're taking you to safety.

70

*SKELLIG struggles to rise from the floor.*

| | |
|---|---|
| **NARRATION** | His joints creaked as he struggled to rise from the floor. |
| **NARRATION** | They felt how thin he was, |
| **NARRATION** | How extraordinarily light he was. |
| **NARRATION** | Their fingers touched behind his back. |
| **NARRATION** | They explored the growths upon his shoulder blades. |
| **NARRATION** | They felt them folded up like arms. |
| **NARRATION** | They felt their soft coverings. |
| **NARRATION** | They stared into each other's eyes, |
| **NARRATION** | And didn't dare to tell each other what they thought they felt. |
| **MINA** | Extraordinary, extraordinary being. |
| **MICHAEL** | Move slowly. Hold on to us. |

*They move out of the garage into the intensifying daylight.*

**NARRATION**      He turned his face away from the intensifying light.

**NARRATION**      They saw for the first time that he wasn't old.

**NARRATION**      He seemed like a young man.

**MINA**      You're beautiful!

**NARRATION**      Already traffic could be heard in the city.

**NARRATION**      The birds yelled their songs.

**NARRATION**      Michael told himself that this was a dream.

**NARRATION**      He told himself that anything was possible in a dream.

**MICHAEL**      We'll carry him!

**MINA**      Yes!

*They carry him.*

**NARRATION**      They carried him through the back lanes,

**NARRATION**      Through the DANGER door.

| | |
|---|---|
| **NARRATION** | They laid him there, in the darkness. |
| **NARRATION** | And for a time they paused, |
| **NARRATION** | As if exhausted, |
| **NARRATION** | As if they slept together there, |
| **NARRATION** | Inside the deep deep deepest dark. |

*MICHAEL gasps in surprise, as if suddenly waking.*

| | |
|---|---|
| **MICHAEL** | My dad! He'll wake up soon. I have to go back. |
| **MINA** | You're safe now. |
| **SKELLIG** | Knackered. Sick to death. Aspirin. |

*MICHAEL feeds SKELLIG aspirin.*

| | |
|---|---|
| **MINA** | We'll make you well now. Is there anything you need? |
| **MICHAEL** | 27 and 53. |
| **SKELLIG** | 27 and 53. |

*MINA kisses SKELLIG. She stretches her arms once more around his back.*

**MINA**          What are you?

*SKELLIG shakes his head. On all fours, he begins to crawl away from her.*

**SKELLIG**          Nothing. Nothing.

**MINA**          Let us help you. I'll make you more comfortable.

*She begins to pull his jacket down over his shoulders.*

**NARRATION**          She slid the jacket over his arms.

**SKELLIG**          No. No!

**MINA**          Trust me.

**NARRATION**          She took the jacket right off him.

**NARRATION**          They saw what both of them had dreamed they would see.

**NARRATION**          Beneath his jacket were wings that grew out through rips in his shirt.

**NARRATION**          The wings began to unfurl from his shoulder blades.

**NARRATION**          They were twisted and uneven.

**NARRATION**          They were covered in cracked and crooked feathers.

| | |
|---|---|
| **NARRATION** | They clicked and trembled as they opened. |
| **NARRATION** | They were wider than his shoulders, higher than his head. |
| **NARRATION** | He whimpered with pain. |
| **NARRATION** | His tears fell. |
| **NARRATION** | They reached out to touch. |
| **MINA** | You're beautiful! |
| **SKELLIG** | Let me sleep. Let me go home. |
| **NARRATION** | He lay face down. |
| **NARRATION** | His wings continued to quiver into life above him. |
| **NARRATION** | They touched them. |
| **NARRATION** | They felt the feathers, |
| **NARRATION** | And beneath them the bones and sinews and muscles that supported them. |
| **NARRATION** | They felt the trembling of his heart. |

| | |
|---|---|
| **NARRATION** | They felt the crackle of his breathing. |
| **MINA** | Oh, what are you? Who are you? Who? |
| **SKELLIG** | My name is Skellig. |

2

*The hospital. The baby is in a glass case.*

| | |
|---|---|
| **NARRATION** | In hospital. |
| **NARRATION** | The wires and tubes were in her. |
| **NARRATION** | The glass case was shut. |
| **NARRATION** | She was wrapped in white. |
| **NARRATION** | Her little hands were clenched tight on either side of her head. |
| **NARRATION** | Michael listened to the drone of the city, |
| **NARRATION** | The clatter of the hospital, |
| **NARRATION** | His own breathing, |
| **NARRATION** | The scared quick breathing of his parents at his side. |

| | |
|---|---|
| **NARRATION** | He listened deeper, |
| **NARRATION** | Until he heard the baby, |
| **NARRATION** | The gentle squeaking of her breath, |
| **NARRATION** | Tiny and distant as if it came from a different world. |
| **NARRATION** | He listened until he heard her beating heart. |
| **NARRATION** | He told himself that if he listened hard enough, |
| **NARRATION** | Her breath and her heart would never be able to stop. |

*MICHAEL holds his heart, backs away.*

| | |
|---|---|
| **NARRATION** | And he went to Mina, once again. |

### 3

*MINA's garden. MICHAEL and MINA sit beneath the tree. MINA has a heavy encyclopaedia. She has a clay model of the archaeopteryx, that she guides through the air as she talks. MICHAEL holds his heart as he listens.*

| MINA | Here it is. Archaeopteryx. The dinosaur that flew. We believe that dinosaurs became extinct. But there's another theory, that their descendants are with us still. They nest in our trees and attics. The air is filled with their songs. The little archaeopteryx survived, and began the line of evolution that led to birds. Wings and feathers, see? But the creature was a heavy, bony thing. Look at the clumsy leaden tail. It was capable of nothing but short, sudden flights. From tree to tree, stone to stone. |

*She imitates the archaeopteryx's thump to earth.*

| MINA | It couldn't rise and spiral and dance like birds can now. |

*She imitates a bird's spiralling flight.*
*The blackbird sings nearby.*

| MINA | If you held the true archaeopteryx, it would be almost as heavy as stone in your hands. It would be almost as heavy as this clay model.<br>There is no end to evolution, Michael. |

|  | Maybe this is not how we are meant to be for ever . . . |
|---|---|
| **MICHAEL** | Mina? |
| **MINA** | Yes. |
| **MICHAEL** | I can feel the baby's heart inside my own. |
| **MINA** | Inside? |
| **MICHAEL** | It's beating beside mine. And I feel her breathing along with me. Feel it, Mina. |

*MINA feels his heart.*

|  |  |
|---|---|
| **MICHAEL** | Can you feel? There. And there. And there. |
| **MINA** | Yes. No. Yes! |
| **MICHAEL** | If I can feel it beating there beside my own, I know the baby's safe. You feel it? |
| **MINA** | Yes. |

*They concentrate together.*

|  |  |
|---|---|
| **MINA** | Yes. Extraordinary. *We* are extraordinary. |

79

**MICHAEL/MINA**   Skellig! Skellig! Skellig!

*MICHAEL and MINA look deep into each other's eyes, lost in the wonder of themselves and of SKELLIG.*

*Then LEAKEY and COOT arrive, and giggle down at them.*

**LEAKEY/COOT**   Ahahahahahah!

4

**NARRATION**   In the street.

**NARRATION**   The football match.

**NARRATION**   And Michael was hopeless, poor lad.

*MICHAEL, LEAKEY and COOT play football. MINA watches from her tree.*

**LEAKEY**   On me head! On me head!

**COOT**   Michael, man! What's wrong with you, man?

**LEAKEY**   It's cos he's been ill.

**COOT**   Bollocks. He's not been ill, he's just been upset.

**MICHAEL**   I'm out of practice.

| | |
|---|---|
| **COOT** | Bollocks. |
| **LEAKEY** | That's right. |
| **COOT** | It's her. Her in the tree. That lass he was with. |
| **LEAKEY** | That's right. |
| **MICHAEL** | Bollocks. |
| **LEAKEY** | It's that lass. |
| **COOT** | That lass that climbs in a tree like a monkey. Her that sits in a tree like a crow. |
| **MICHAEL** | Bollocks. |
| **LEAKEY** | He holds hands with her. |
| **COOT** | She says he's extraordinary. |
| **LEAKEY** | Extraordinary! |
| **MICHAEL** | Get stuffed. |

*MICHAEL moves away from them. He sits against the garage. LEAKEY and COOT follow. LEAKEY sits by MICHAEL, appears sympathetic.*

| | |
|---|---|
| **MICHAEL** | The baby's ill. Really ill. The doctor says I'm in distress |

81

| | |
|---|---|
| **LEAKEY** | Yeah. Yeah, I know. I'm sorry. |
| **LEAKEY** | Who is she, anyway? |
| **MICHAEL** | She's called Mina. |
| **LEAKEY** | What school's she at? |
| **MICHAEL** | She doesn't go to school. |
| **LEAKEY** | Plays the wag, eh? |
| **COOT** | Or is she just too thick? |
| **MICHAEL** | Her mother teaches her. |
| **LEAKEY** | Hell's teeth. Thought you had to go to school. Lucky sod. |
| **COOT** | What'll she do for mates, though? And who'd like to be stuck at home all day? |
| **MICHAEL** | They think schools stop you from learning. They think schools try to make everybody just the same. |
| **COOT** | That's bollocks, that. |
| **LEAKEY** | Aye. You're learning all day long in school. |
| **MICHAEL** | Maybe. |

| | |
|---|---|
| **LEAKEY** | Is that why you've not been coming in? Is it cos you're never coming back again? You're going to let that lass's mother teach you? |
| **MICHAEL** | Course not. But they're going to teach me some things. |
| **LEAKEY** | Like? |
| **MICHAEL** | Like modelling with clay. And about William Blake. |
| **COOT** | Who's he? That bloke that's got the butcher's shop in town? |
| **MICHAEL** | He said school drives all joy away. He was a painter and a poet. |
| **COOT** | Oh, aye? |
| **LEAKEY** | Oh, aye? |
| **MICHAEL** | Look. I can't tell you everything. But the world's full of amazing things. I've seen them . . . |

*COOT catches sight of MINA again.*

| | |
|---|---|
| **COOT** | There she is. |
| **LEAKEY** | The monkey girl. |

| | |
|---|---|
| **COOT** | Hey. Mebbe Rasputin's right about that evolution stuff. He could come and look at her and see there's monkeys all around us still. |

*LEAKEY and COOT run off.*
*MICHAEL turns to MINA.*

| | |
|---|---|
| **MINA** | 'Thank God I was never sent to school,<br>To be flogd into following the style of a Fool.' |
| **MICHAEL** | You know nothing about it. We don't get flogged and my friends aren't fools. |
| **MINA** | Ha! |
| **MICHAEL** | You know nothing about it. You might know about William Blake but you know nothing about what ordinary people do. |
| **MINA** | Ha! |
| **MICHAEL** | Yes. Ha! |
| **MINA** | They hate me. I could see it in their eyes. They think I'm taking you away from them. They're stupid. |

| | |
|---|---|
| **MICHAEL** | They're not stupid! |
| **MINA** | Stupid. Kicking balls and jumping at each other and screeching like hyenas. Stupid. Yes, hyenas! You as well. |
| **MICHAEL** | Hyenas? They think you're a monkey, then. |
| **MINA** | See what I mean? They know nothing about me but they hate me. |
| **MICHAEL** | And of course you know everything about them. |
| **MINA** | There's nothing to know. Kicking, screeching, being stupid. |
| **MICHAEL** | Ha! |
| **MINA** | Yes, ha! And that little ginger one . . . |
| **MICHAEL** | Blake was little and ginger. |
| **MINA** | How do you know that? |
| **MICHAEL** | See? You think nobody but you can know anything. |
| **MINA** | No, I don't. |

| | |
|---|---|
| **MICHAEL** | Ha! |
| **MINA** | Go home. Go and play stupid football or something. Leave me alone. |

*MICHAEL runs from her in torment. He plays football alone with a desperate energy. DAD appears.*

| | |
|---|---|
| **DAD** | Michael. Michael! |

*MICHAEL looks at him, doesn't respond.*

| | |
|---|---|
| **DAD** | You can tell me, son. Come on, eh? |
| **MICHAEL** | Leave me alone! There's nothing to tell. There's nothing to bloody tell! |

### 5

*Night. MICHAEL's bedroom. Owls hoot. MICHAEL wakes, dresses, leaves.*

| | |
|---|---|
| **NARRATION** | The owls woke him that night. |
| **NARRATION** | Or a call that was like that of the owls. |
| **NARRATION** | The moon hung over the city. |

| | |
|---|---|
| **NARRATION** | He went out into the dark. |
| **NARRATION** | He walked through the deep shadows towards the DANGER house. |

*He finds MINA on the doorstep.*

| | |
|---|---|
| **MINA** | What took so long? Thought I was going to have to do this all alone. |
| **MICHAEL** | Thought that was what you wanted. |
| **MINA** | Oh, Michael. We said stupid things. I said stupid things. |

*An owl hoots.*

| | |
|---|---|
| **MINA** | Don't be angry. Be my friend. |
| **MICHAEL** | I am your friend. |
| **MINA** | It's possible to hate your friend. You hated me today. |
| **MICHAEL** | You hated me. |
| **MINA** | I love the night. Anything seems possible at night when the rest of the world has gone to sleep. Oh, Michael, let's go inside. |
| **MICHAEL** | Yes, let's go inside. |

87

| | |
|---|---|
| **NARRATION** | So they stepped again through the DANGER door. |
| **NARRATION** | They blundered through the dark. |
| **NARRATION** | They found nothing. |
| **MINA** | Where is he? |
| **MICHAEL** | Skellig! |
| **MINA** | Skellig! |
| **NARRATION** | Their hearts thundered. |
| **MICHAEL** | Where is he? |
| **NARRATION** | They stumbled up the stairs. |
| **MICHAEL** | Skellig! |
| **MINA** | Skellig! |
| **NARRATION** | No answer. |
| **NARRATION** | Their heads were filled with the darkness of the house. |
| **MINA** | Stand still. Listen to the deepest deepest places of the dark. |
| **NARRATION** | They held hands. |

| | |
|---|---|
| **NARRATION** | They listened to the night. |
| **NARRATION** | Michael heard the breathing of the baby deep inside himself. |
| **NARRATION** | He heard the far-off beating of her heart. |
| **NARRATION** | They listened to the deepest places of the dark. |
| **NARRATION** | It came from above them. |
| **MINA** | You hear? |
| **MICHAEL** | Yes! |
| **MINA** | Skellig's breathing! |
| **NARRATION** | They climbed the final flight of stairs. |
| **NARRATION** | Towards the final doorway. |
| **NARRATION** | Gently, fearfully, they opened the door. |
| **NARRATION** | They saw his silhouette against the arched window. |
| **NARRATION** | They saw the silhouette of his wings folded upon his shoulders. |

| | |
|---|---|
| **NARRATION** | They didn't dare approach him. |
| **NARRATION** | And as they watched, an owl appeared, |
| **NARRATION** | Dropping on silent wings from the moonlit sky to the moonlit window. |
| **NARRATION** | It laid something on the window sill, |
| **NARRATION** | And flew off again. |
| **NARRATION** | Skellig bent his head to where the bird had been. |
| **NARRATION** | And he ate the thing that had been left there. |
| **MINA** | They're feeding him! |
| **NARRATION** | And then he turned to them. |
| **SKELLIG** | Come to me. |

*They don't move.*

| | |
|---|---|
| **SKELLIG** | Come to me. |

*They go to him. He takes their hands.*

**SKELLIG**     Take my hand.

*They make a circle.*

**NARRATION**     Michael caught the stench of
Skellig's breath.

**NARRATION**     His breath was the breath of an
animal that lives on the meat of
other living things.

**NARRATION**     A dog.

**NARRATION**     A fox.

**NARRATION**     A blackbird.

**NARRATION**     An owl.

**NARRATION**     He stepped sideways and they
turned together,

**NARRATION**     And kept slowly turning

**NARRATION**     As if they were carefully,
nervously,

**NARRATION**     Beginning to dance.

*They turn. MICHAEL holds back.*

**SKELLIG**     Don't stop, Michael.

| | |
|---|---|
| **MINA** | No, Michael. Don't stop! |
| **NARRATION** | He didn't stop. |
| **NARRATION** | He felt Skellig's and Mina's hearts beating alongside his own. |
| **NARRATION** | He felt their breath in rhythm with his. |
| **NARRATION** | It was as if they moved into each other, |
| **NARRATION** | As if they became one thing. |
| **NARRATION** | And for a moment he saw ghostly wings at Mina's back. |
| **NARRATION** | He felt feathers and delicate bones rising from his own shoulders. |
| **NARRATION** | And he was lifted from the floor with Skellig and Mina. |
| **NARRATION** | They turned circles together through the empty air of that empty room |
| **NARRATION** | High in an old house in Crow Road . . . |
| **NARRATION** | And then it was over. |

*They return to the floor. SKELLIG touches the children's heads.*

**SKELLIG**     Go home now.

**MICHAEL**     But how are you like this now?

**SKELLIG**     The owls and the angels.
Remember this night.
Remember this night.

**NARRATION**     They stepped back out together into the night.

**NARRATION**     They hurried homeward, filled with joy . . .

**NARRATION**     And next day things just started to go wrong.

**NARRATION**     So wrong.

**NARRATION**     Poor Michael.

6

*In school.*

**NARRATION**     In school,

**NARRATION**     The lessons continued,

**NARRATION**    The football continued,

**NARRATION**    The writing continued.

*RASPUTIN has a long poster of a cut-away person: lungs, heart etc. all exposed.*

**RASPUTIN**    Here we are. Our dark interior. This is what all of our evolution has been leading to. The inner us.

**COOT**    Ugh!

**RASPUTIN**    Yes, Mr Coot. Even the inner you. Come here.

*He beckons COOT towards him, acts out stripping away COOT's skin, tearing open his chest.*

**RASPUTIN**    Yes. Inside we're all the same, no matter how horrible the outside might be. This is what we would see were we to open up our Mr Coot.

*COOT scuttles back to his desk.*

**RASPUTIN**    Now, I'd like you to place your hand on your chest like this. Feel the beating of your heart. This is our engine, beating day and night. Mostly we're hardly aware that it's even there. But if it stopped . . .

*C*OOT *squawks and pretends to die.*

**RASPUTIN**        Correct, Mr Coot.

*R*ASPUTIN, *too, flops across his desk as if dead. Others copy.* M*ICHAEL* *holds his heart, looks around him in fright.*

*Football.* M*ICHAEL* *plays with a desperate energy.*

**MICHAEL**        On me head! On me head! Yeah!

*The others watch him in amazement and admiration.*

**LEAKEY**        Give it to Michael! Go on!

**COOT**        Look at him. He's even better
                than he was before!

**MICHAEL**        On me head! On me bloody
                head!

*An English lesson with* M*ISS* C*LARTS. **She has been
reading a story by* M*ICHAEL.*

**MISS CLARTS**        Oh, Michael, your style is really
                coming on. And such an
                imagination.

*She addresses the class.*

**MISS CLARTS**        A boy finds an old stinking tramp
                in a warehouse by the river who
                turns out to have wings under his

95

ancient coat. The boy feeds the man with sandwiches and chocolate and the man becomes strong again. The man teaches the boy and his friend Kara how to fly . . .

'We moved faster and faster until I felt myself being lifted from the floor. I left all my troubles behind . . .' How do you come up with such things, Michael?

*RASPUTIN cuts in.*

**RASPUTIN**     Michael . . . Your dad's been on the phone, Michael.

*MICHAEL gasps, turns.*

**RASPUTIN**     Says he's been held up at the hospital. Says can you go to . . . is it Mina's? . . . for your tea. It's OK. It's just routine, he says.

*MICHAEL backs away, holds his heart.*

**RASPUTIN**     Michael?

**MICHAEL**     I should have stayed at home. I should have kept on thinking about her.

**RASPUTIN**     Michael?

96

**MISS CLARTS**     Michael?

*MICHAEL backs away.*


### 7


**NARRATION**     In Mina's house.

*MINA's house. MINA and MICHAEL are at the kitchen table with paints and paper. MRS MCKEE is preparing food. MINA has drawn a large picture of SKELLIG.*

**MRS McKEE**     It's lovely, isn't it, Michael?

**MICHAEL**     Yes.

**MRS McKEE**     The kind of thing William Blake saw. He said we were surrounded by angels and spirits, we must just open our eyes a little wider, look a little harder . . . But it's enough for me to have you two angels at my table. Isn't it amazing? I see you clearly, two angels at my table.

*MICHAEL draws with energy.*
*MRS MCKEE sings.*


**MRS McKEE**     'I dreamt a dream! What can it mean?
And that I was a maiden Queen . . .'

| | |
|---|---|
| **MINA** | I went to Skellig today. |
| **MRS McKEE** | 'Guarded by an Angel mild<br>Witless woe, was ne'er beguiled!' |
| **MINA** | Skellig said, Where's Michael? At school, I said.<br>School! He said. He abandons me for school! I said you hadn't abandoned him. I said you loved him. |
| **MICHAEL** | I do. |
| **MINA** | He says you must keep coming to see him.<br>He says he's going away soon, Michael. |
| **MRS McKEE** | 'So he took his wings and fled:<br>Then the morn blush'd rosy red . . .' |
| **MICHAEL** | Going away? |
| **MINA** | Yes. |
| **MICHAEL** | Where to? |
| **MINA** | He wouldn't say. |
| **MICHAEL** | When? |

**MINA**              Soon.

**MRS McKEE**         'Soon my Angel came again;
                      I was armed, he came in vain . . .'

*MRS MCKEE leans over the children, clearing a space on the table.*

**MRS McKEE**         'For the time of youth was fled,
                      And grey hairs were on my head.'
                      Come on. Bunk up. Food's
                      ready. That's a lovely picture,
                      Michael.

*The telephone rings. MRS MCKEE answers.*

**MRS McKEE**         It's your dad, Michael.

*He doesn't move.*

**MRS McKEE**         Michael.

*In dread, MICHAEL takes the phone.*

**MICHAEL**           Dad?
                      Tomorrow. What do you mean,
                      tomorrow?
                      Operate? What they going to do?
                      Dad, what they going to do?

*MICHAEL drops the phone.*

| | |
|---|---|
| **MICHAEL** | Her heart . . . They're operating on her heart. |

*MICHAEL holds his hands to his heart.*

## 8

| | |
|---|---|
| **NARRATION** | That night was endless. |
| **NARRATION** | In and out of sleep. |
| **NARRATION** | In and out of dreadful dreams. |
| **NARRATION** | No moon in the sky. |
| **NARRATION** | The clocks were surely stuck. |
| **NARRATION** | Then true sleep must have come at last. |
| **NARRATION** | And Michael woke to daylight with stinging eyes and sunken heart. |

*In the kitchen. Morning.*

| | |
|---|---|
| **MICHAEL** | No! I won't go to school! Why should I? Not today! |
| **DAD** | You'll do as you're bloody told. You'll do what's best for your mum and the baby. |

| | |
|---|---|
| **MICHAEL** | You just want me out of the way so you don't have to think about me and don't have to worry about me and you can just think about the bloody baby! |
| **DAD** | Don't say bloody! |
| **MICHAEL** | It is bloody! It's bloody bloody bloody! And it isn't fair! |

*DAD kicks the table. Milk and jam crash to the floor.*

| | |
|---|---|
| **DAD** | See? See the state you get me in? Go to bloody school! Get out my bloody sight!<br>I love you. I love you. |

*They hold each other.*

| | |
|---|---|
| **DAD** | You could come, Michael. But there'd be nothing you could do. We just have to wait and pray and believe that everything will be all right. |

*MINA comes to the door. MICHAEL answers the bell.*

| | |
|---|---|
| **MINA** | You've got to come to help me. You've got to help me protect them. |

101

DAD

I'll come for you this afternoon, when the operation's over. Go with Mina. Keep believing.

9

*MINA'S front garden. The blackbird calls its warning sound.*

MINA

The fledglings are out. Stay dead still and dead quiet. Watch out for cats. Send them off. Sssss! Look under the hedge. Look under the rose tree by the wall. Little brown feathered balls. Can you see them?

MICHAEL

Yes.

MINA

So exposed. So all alone. They're out of the nest. They can't fly. Their parents still have to feed them. All they can do is totter and tremble and hide in the shadows and wait for their food. They're in such peril.
They'll be doing this all day, flying and feeding all the way till dusk. And the same thing tomorrow and tomorrow till the chicks can fly.

102

Cats want them. And crows. And
stupid dogs. They're so exposed.
So all alone. Death is all around
them.
Sit tight, Michael. Sit still and
look over them.

*MRS McKEE comes to MICHAEL and MINA.*

**MRS McKEE**    Hello, you two. Thought you
might like some of this.

*She's carrying a pomegranate in quarters. She passes them
around, and pins with which to pick out the seeds.*

**MINA**    Pomegranates. Lovely.

**MRS McKEE**    Pomegranate. Isn't it a lovely
word? Look at all the life in it.
Every pip could become a tree
and every tree could bear a
thousand fruits and every fruit
could bear another thousand
trees.

**MINA**    And if every seed became a tree,
there'd be no room in the world
for anything but pomegranate
trees.

**MRS McKEE**    It's what Persephone ate when
she was waiting in the
Underworld.

103

**MICHAEL**          Who's Persephone?

**MRS McKEE**          The goddess of the spring. She is forced to spend half the year in darkness deep underground. It's winter then – the days are cold and short and dark. Living things hide themselves away. They even seem to die. Then she's released. She makes her slow way back up to the world again. The world gets brighter and bolder to welcome her back. Light and heat. Living things sense her approach. The animals dare to wake. They dare to have their young. Plants send out buds and shoots. Life dares to come back again. Spring comes back to the world.

**MICHAEL**          An old myth. A story for ancient people and for little kids.

**MRS McKEE**          But maybe it's a myth that's nearly true. Look around you, Michael. Fledglings, blooms, bright sunshine. Maybe what we see around us is the whole world welcoming Persephone home . . . They can do marvellous things,

Michael. Maybe you'll soon be welcoming your own Persephone home.

*They dream of Persephone's slow and perilous journey back towards the surface of the world.*

**MRS McKEE**     I'll watch the birds. Why not go and wander for a while?

*MICHAEL and MINA walk.*

**NARRATION**     It was like walking in a dream.

**NARRATION**     The sun glared over the rooftops.

**NARRATION**     Birds were ragged and black against the astonishing sky.

**NARRATION**     The roadway glistened, a deep black pond.

**NARRATION**     Mina led him towards the DANGER door.

**NARRATION**     They entered in silence.

**NARRATION**     They went up in silence.

*They pause.*

**MINA**     He'll be waiting for us, Michael. He'll be so pleased to see you again.

**NARRATION**     She led him into the attic.

105

| | |
|---|---|
| **MINA** | Not here!<br>Skellig! Skellig! Skellig! |
| **NARRATION** | She searched the house. |
| **NARRATION** | He wasn't there. |
| **MINA** | He isn't here at all. |

*MICHAEL clutches his heart.*

| | |
|---|---|
| **MICHAEL** | Oh, Mina! |
| **MINA** | What is it? |
| **MICHAEL** | My heart's stopped. Feel my<br>heart. There's nothing there. |

*He faints, falls. MINA touches his heart.*

| | |
|---|---|
| **MINA** | But I can feel it. There and there<br>and there. |
| **MICHAEL** | But it's only my heart. It's not the<br>baby's. |
| **MINA** | Oh, Michael. |
| **MICHAEL** | It's only mine. Not the baby's.<br>The baby's dead. |
| **MINA** | You can't know for certain. |
| **MICHAEL** | She's dead. Where is he? Skellig!<br>Skellig! Where the hell are you?<br>Skellig! |

| | |
|---|---|
| **MINA** | Don't, Michael. |
| **MICHAEL** | Maybe he's gone away for ever, like he said he would. |
| **MICHAEL** | Maybe he was never even here at all! |
| **MINA** | Skellig! Skellig! Bloody Skellig! |

*DAD calls from outside.*

| | |
|---|---|
| **DAD** | Michael! Michael! Michael! |

*MICHAEL gasps in fright.*

| | |
|---|---|
| **MINA** | Come on, Michael. |

*MICHAEL doesn't move.*

| | |
|---|---|
| **MINA** | Come on. |

*They leave the house. They meet DAD outside.*

| | |
|---|---|
| **DAD** | It's over, son. |

### 10

| | |
|---|---|
| **NARRATION** | Michael was wrong. |
| **NARRATION** | She wasn't dead. |
| **NARRATION** | She was snoring gently. |

107

**NARRATION**    Her little hands were clenched beside her head.

*The hospital. A machine bleeps in rhythm with the baby's heart.*

**MUM**    They said she has a heart of fire. They said there was a moment when they thought they'd lost her. But she burst into life again. Wouldn't give in.

**DAD**    We haven't even named her yet.

**MICHAEL**    Persephone.

**DAD**    Bit of a mouthful, eh?

**MUM**    It was the strangest thing.

**DAD**    What was?

**MUM**    Well, I was lying here last night, tossing and turning. Kept getting up to look at her. Kept dropping off to sleep. And the strangest of dreams . . .

**DAD**    And . . . ?

**MUM**    And I saw this man. Another dream, though I was sure I was wide awake. He was standing over the baby. He was filthy. All

108

in black, an ancient dusty suit. A great hunch on his back. Hair all matted and tangled. I was terrified. I wanted to reach out to him. I wanted to push him away. I wanted to scream, Get away from our baby! I wanted to shout for the nurses and doctors. But I couldn't move, couldn't speak, and I was sure he was going to take her away. But then he turned and looked at me. His face as dry and white as chalk. And such tenderness in his eyes. And for some reason I knew he hadn't come to harm her. I knew it would be all right . . .

**DAD**            And . . . ?

**MUM**            And then he reached right down with both hands and lifted her up. She was wide awake. They stared and stared into each other's eyes. He started to slowly turn around . . .

**MICHAEL**        Like they were dancing.

**MUM**            That's right. Like they were dancing. And then the strangest

109

thing of all . . . The strangest thing of all, there were wings on the baby's back. Not solid wings. Transparent, ghostly, hardly visible, but there they were. Little feathery things. It looked so funny. The strange tall man and the little baby and the wings. And that was it. He put her back down, he turned and looked at me again, and it was over. I slept like a log the rest of the night. When I woke they were already getting her ready for the operation. But I wasn't worried any more. I kissed her and whispered to her how much we all loved her and they took her away. I knew it was going to be all right.

**DAD**   And it is.

**MUM**   And it is.
I must have been thinking about what you asked me.
What are shoulder blades for?
Eh?

**MICHAEL**   Yes. Yes.

| | |
|---|---|
| **MUM** | It isn't over. You know that, don't you? We'll have to protect her always, especially at first. |
| **MICHAEL** | I know that. We'll love her and love her and love her. |

*DAD and MICHAEL prepare to leave.*

| | |
|---|---|
| **MICHAEL** | See you tomorrow, Mum. See you tomorrow, little chick. |

*As they leave, MICHAEL sees DR MACNABOLA with a clutch of students around him. MICHAEL hurries to him.*

| | |
|---|---|
| **MICHAEL** | Doctor MacNabola. |
| **DR MACNABOLA** | Yes. |
| **MICHAEL** | I told you about my friend. The one with arthritis. |
| **DR MACNABOLA** | Aha. So is he ready for my needles and saw? |
| **MICHAEL** | He seems to be getting better. |
| **DR MACNABOLA** | Splendid. Maybe he'll escape me yet. |
| **MICHAEL** | Doctor? |
| **DR MACNABOLA** | Yes? |

| | |
|---|---|
| **MICHAEL** | Can love help a person to get better? |
| **DR MacNABOLA** | Love. What can we doctors know about love?<br>'Love is the child that breathes our breath,<br>Love is the child that scatters death.' |
| **MICHAEL** | William Blake? |
| **DR MacNABOLA** | We have an educated man before us.<br>Tell your friend that I hope he and I never have to meet. |

*DR MacNABOLA moves on. MICHAEL goes back to DAD.*

| | |
|---|---|
| **DAD** | What was that all about? |
| **MICHAEL** | Just somebody I met soon after the baby came in. |
| **DAD** | Mystery man, that's you.<br>She's not out of danger yet. You understand that, don't you? |
| **MICHAEL** | Yes. But she will be, won't she? |
| **DAD** | Yes! Yes, she blinking will!<br>Hey, I know. We could have 27 and 53 tonight, eh? |
| **MICHAEL** | 27 and 53. Sweetest of nectars. |

| | |
|---|---|
| **DAD** | Sweetest of nectars. I like that. Sweetest of blinking nectars! |

## 11

*In the DANGER house. Night.*

| | |
|---|---|
| **NARRATION** | They went once more through the DANGER door. |
| **NARRATION** | Once more into the attic. |
| **NARRATION** | It was empty, dark and silent. |
| **NARRATION** | They took 27 and 53 and brown ale. |
| **NARRATION** | But there was no Skellig. |
| **MINA** | He isn't here at all. Ah, well. |
| **MICHAEL** | Feel my heart, Mina. Can you feel it? Her heart beating right inside there beside my own. |

*MINA touches his heart.*

| | |
|---|---|
| **MICHAEL** | It's like touching and listening and imagining all at the same time. It's like blackbird chicks cheeping in a nest. |

113

| | |
|---|---|
| **MINA** | Yes. Yes, there it is. There and there and there. |
| **MICHAEL** | The baby's heart. It won't stop now. |
| **MINA** | It won't stop now. I could sleep here. Just like this. And be happy for ever. |
| **MICHAEL** | Yes. But we have to go. |
| **NARRATION** | They didn't move. |
| **NARRATION** | And there came a rustling in the air outside. |
| **NARRATION** | The stars were blocked out. |
| **NARRATION** | The window creaked. |
| **NARRATION** | And there he was, climbing in through the arched window. |
| **NARRATION** | He crouched there, gasping for breath. |
| **NARRATION** | His wings slowly settled on his back. |
| **MICHAEL** | Skellig. |
| **SKELLIG** | Michael. Mina. |

| | |
|---|---|
| **MICHAEL** | We brought you this, Skellig. 27 and 53. |
| **SKELLIG** | Ha! |

*They crouch at his side and hold out the food. He slurps and licks and groans.*

| | |
|---|---|
| **SKELLIG** | Sweetest of nectars. Food of the blinking gods. |
| **MICHAEL** | And this. |

*He snaps the top off the brown ale and gives it to SKELLIG. He drinks.*

| | |
|---|---|
| **SKELLIG** | Thought it was cold mice for supper and I come home to a banquet.<br>Pair of angels, that's what you are. |
| **MICHAEL** | You went to my sister. |
| **SKELLIG** | Hm! Lovely thing. |
| **MICHAEL** | You made her strong. |
| **SKELLIG** | That one's glittering with life. Heart like fire. It was her that gave the strength to me.<br>But worn out now. Knackered. |

*He reaches out and touches MINA and MICHAEL's faces.*

115

**SKELLIG**          But I'm getting strong, thanks to the angels and the owls.

**MICHAEL**        You're going away.

*SKELLIG nods.*

**MICHAEL**        Where will you go?

**SKELLIG**          Somewhere.

*MICHAEL touches him.*

**MICHAEL**        What are you, Skellig?

**SKELLIG**          Something. Something like you, something like a beast, something like a bird, something like an angel. Something like that.
Let's stand up.

*They make a circle, holding hands.*

**NARRATION**     They made their circle.

**NARRATION**     They looked deep into each other's eyes,

**NARRATION**     And they held each other tight.

**NARRATION**     Their hearts beat as one.

**NARRATION**     They breathed as one.

| | |
|---|---|
| **NARRATION** | They danced. |
| **NARRATION** | They turned once more in the empty air |
| **NARRATION** | And ghostly wings rose from Michael's and Mina's backs. |
| **NARRATION** | And then it ended, and they came to earth again. |
| **MINA** | We'll remember for ever. |

*Skellig hugs them both.*

| | |
|---|---|
| **SKELLIG** | Thank you for 27 and 53. Thank you for giving me my life again. Now you have to go home. |
| **NARRATION** | And so they left the attic. |
| **NARRATION** | And went down through the DANGER house. |
| **NARRATION** | And they stepped together into the astounding night. |

### 12

*The kitchen. Morning.*

| | |
|---|---|
| **NARRATION** | It was really spring at last. |

| | |
|---|---|
| **NARRATION** | On a bright morning, the baby with the mended heart was carried from the hospital, |
| **NARRATION** | And she was brought back home to Falconer Road. |
| **NARRATION** | And her mum and her dad and her brother Michael sat around her, |
| **NARRATION** | And looked at her in wonder. |
| **NARRATION** | They laughed and laughed, |
| **NARRATION** | And cried and cried. |
| **NARRATION** | And they asked themselves, |
| **DAD** | So, what shall we call her? |
| **MUM** | Joy. |
| **DAD** | Eh? |
| **MUM** | Joy. We'll call her Joy. |